The Death Curl

Raven Amburgey

BookLeaf Publishing

India | USA | UK

Presentation by *BookLeaf Publishing*

Web: www.bookleafpub.com

E-mail: info@bookleafpub.com

ISBN: 9789360945015

First edition 2024

ACKNOWLEDGEMENT

I extend my sincere gratitude to *The Cincinnati Fiction Writers* group and *The Southwest Ohio Writer's Club*. Through their invaluable support, which manifests both as rigorous critique sessions and simple socials to unwind and encourage creative juices to flow, they have played an indispensable role in shaping my journey as a writer.

Membership in these groups brought not only challenges but also the profound gift of finding a community that feels like home. In them, I discovered "my people." The privilege of choosing a second family is a unique and cherished blessing.

I am deeply grateful for the guidance, encouragement, and camaraderie they have provided, all of which have been instrumental in my growth and development as a writer. Their influence has been as significant as the hours spent at my keyboard and the determination that fuels my journey. I owe them a debt of gratitude for their unwavering support and belief in my potential. Sometimes, that's what brings these projects to reality.

PREFACE

Welcome to *The Death Curl*. Before delving into its pages, we would like to extend a gentle reminder. This collection of poems delves into sensitive topics that may evoke strong emotions in some readers. Themes such as toxic relationships, disordered eating, rape/sexual assault, substance abuse, negative body image, and animal death are explored within these verses.

If you suspect that any of these subjects may trigger discomfort or distress, or if you are sensitive to mild language, we encourage you to approach this book with caution, mindfulness, and self-awareness. Your mental well-being is paramount. It's perfectly acceptable to pause, to reflect, or even to set this book aside if needed. Remember, knowing your own boundaries is an act of self-care.

Thank you for considering these words as you embark on this literary journey.

The Death Curl

When the tarantula approaches expiry, he
experiences a phenomenon known as
"the death curl."
The tarantula makes himself small.
      The pressure inside his body drops.
He curls his legs into his abdomen.
      Frail and fightless, he waits for death.
It's not to be mistaken for a molt
      in which he lays on his back,
         belly exposed to the world,
            ready to shed his past.
He's given up.
      All pain.
         All life.
            All hope.

When I approached the absence of you, I
experienced a death curl of my own.
Like a fetus,
            you made me small,
curled inward on my half-sheeted mattress.
Too exhausted to invite it in myself, I waited for
death.
It was not to be mistaken for commencement,
in which a bright new chapter opens before
me—
where I openly welcome the next kick off from
another suitor.
I simply couldn't shed you.
I'd given up.
            All pain.
                    All life.
                            All hope.
But one day, a stranger strolled past and offered
me a glass of water.
            Its cold shocked my body to a start.
The ice clanking against my sensitive teeth irked
me *just* enough
            that I sat up.
It was uncomfortable at first,
but I soon realized
I was, in fact, very thirsty.
So, I asked for just a little more.
Even though it was void of flavor,
            I drank it up

more and more
until I realized
I like water.

Not long after that,
I learned that the tarantula experiences a death
curl also when he is dehydrated.
So, I perked up.
I felt the pain.
I experienced life.
I began to hope.

For Jericho

Do not hide, my son,
        behind the veil of social delicacies
        or the wall of peaceable platitudes.
Raise Hell
to anyone who mocks your love of math or
science
or your wondrous gaze on the patterning of stars
hung in a country sky.
These stars were hung for you.
Do not weep, my love,
        behind the glasses you hate to wear
and fling upon your nightstand with disdain.
"Four eyes" means you see the most.

Glasses protect and guide the beauteous orbs I
so adore;
Those eyes which belong to neither your mother
nor father,
      but are distinctly yours alone.
Do not be silent, Darling,
      when you are called upon to sing.
Belt shamelessly for the joy of it.
      Hit the notes or don't…but *sing*.
Do not, do not, do not.
      I can say these words all day.
But what you see is what you'll be.
Do look to me, my boy.
Look at the one who loves you so
for all the nooks and crannies of your soul.
Do look in the mirror and smile.
      Do hug with all your might.
          Do dance when watched or not.
Do be you, Sweetheart,
      In every way God made you to be.
Be you, and love you,
      as you know that I do too.
For diamonds are not precious
      for their dazzle or their strength;
It's rarity that makes their worth,
      and there's no one in the world like you.

Corrosive Plastic

There's a bag of bags I keep in my kitchen.
    My great granny had one too.
It's gotten over-crowded,
    and it's bursting at the side…
But I know that just *one* more will always fit.
    I can make some room.
I just can't bring myself to throw away the
plastic,
    knowing the damage it can do.
But more than this, I convince myself it has a
purpose.
    It has value.
      It has place.
Someday, someday…I'll be glad I made the
space.
There's a man I keep in my heart,
    although he does not love me too.

It's gotten very small in here,
        and there's less of me each day…
But I still have a bag of bags in the kitchen,
        and sleep alone in my own bedroom.
I just can't bring myself to let him go,
        despite the water flooding the bridge.
I convince myself, there is a purpose;
        There is some value
                if I allow him just a little grace
                    Someday, someday…

Helpful Advice

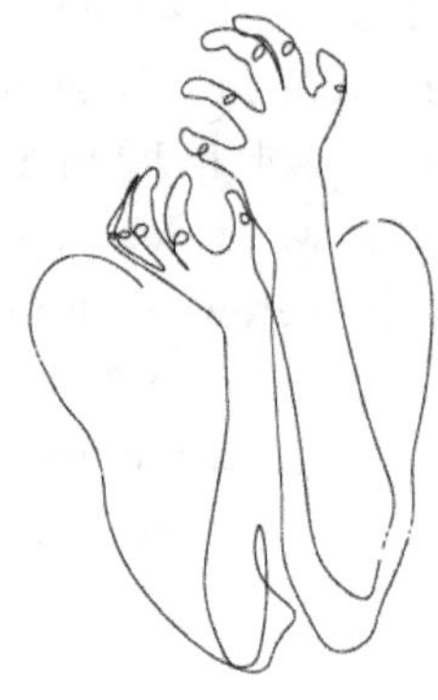

There's a tiny woman deep inside my body;
She tells me what to eat,
whom to trust.
She desperately wants out.
It isn't that I don't trust her judgment—
Calorie-deficits *do* shed pounds.
A beautiful partner *couldn't* worship this body as
I do hers.
She's desperate, but maybe she's right.
I keep her inside, my little prisoner to guide me.
Still, no matter what I do,
Her pleas never bring me success.
Afterall, she's only trying to escape.
But this big woman, who *is* my body—
the one who douses her rice in cilantro and
butter

and shoots her shot at beautiful girls—
I think she's a bit of alright.
So, I keep her on the outside, even though she's
still afraid to take the reins.
      She listens to the nag within,
         and she's afraid of her success.
She just wants to be herself.
She *needs* to be herself.

Proper Hostess

Nobody wants to wash the dishes
        after a delicious holiday feast.
People love to carve the tender cuts of spiral
ham,
        section the flaky fresh-baked pies,
                and sneak an extra deviled egg
or two when no one's watching.
Like any welcoming hostess,
I try to make sure there's something for
everyone.
Anna's kid can't have peanuts.
        Sue's a vegetarian.
                Bob has acid reflux.
I make so many exception dishes that before I
realize it,
        my fire alarm is ringing,
                my countertops are full,

and I've nowhere to put the gluten-free cookies I
just pulled out.
Both hands are full of steaming sheet pans,
there's a toddler yanking on my apron asking for
juice,
       and the alarm is *still* going off.
The cat is about to jump on the countertop with
the ham,
Bob isn't using a coaster on my wooden end
table,
and someone's kid left a cup of milk on the edge
of the bookshelf.
But I can handle this.
       One thing at a time.
        It's the duty of a gracious host.
Susan, can I top off your tea?
Ella, do you want to watch *Scooby Doo*?
Oh, Marvin, Honey, your fly is unzipped.
I weave through everyone, checking for smiles,
exchanging pleasantries and taking plates,
       and it's become a form of art—
like a waltz I've classically trained for years to
prepare for.
Everyone loves watching a graceful dancer,
and so many have an input about how it could be
done better.
       That was a rough transition.
        Her posture was too lax.
But who can realistically do it better?

I complete my performance with few technical
errors,
I make my many efforts to accommodate each
guest,
          and then, the party's over.
And here are all the dishes.
Guests are happy to take leftovers.
Guests are happy to point out the meat was too
dry.
But here are all the dishes.
My back is aching from the bends and twists of
prepping and cooking,
my hair is frizzy, stuck to my forehead, and half
out of its scrunchie,
and the cat has just succeeded at snatching a
paw-full of ham.
And here are all the dishes.
I give,
          and I give,
                    and I give,
and I *still* wash the dishes.
This made me realize that I'm hostess to my
own life,
making exceptions for anyone else
uncomfortable,
and bending over backwards for people I don't
even like.
Oh, I'm sorry. Was I too loud?
I can change the program if you don't like it.

Do you want me to cover the ticket to this band *I*
invited *you* to see?
Sure, I can come in on my day off.
I give,
      and I give,
            and I give.
Someone else can wash the fucking dishes.

Dumpling

A dumpling is a lump of dough
      prepared by simmering or steaming,
often stuffed with sweet or savory filling.
Buoyant and beige,
      their substance dense,
they're perfect for a Thanksgiving feast.
So, one November,
      I slaved over a swollen belly,
         and I brewed myself a baby.
I called him "My Little Teddy Dumpling."
I watched his chubby cheeks, like lumps of
dough,
preparing themselves for their first smile,
      deliver the grumpiest scowl instead.
Balding but blonde,
I slaved over his cradle cap,
with every home remedy he'd let me use.

And by Christmas,
        it was almost all gone—
                Mommy's shiny-headed boy.
Every chef shows off his dish
        with the best of presentations
                and the finest garnish
and colors complimentary to the course.
And how I showed him off,
        My Little Teddy Dumpling,
with every cute teddy bear prop and blankie
        and baby blues to match his too.
But all chef's dishes come to pass,
        especially ones too good to flaut.
He's no longer My Little Teddy Dumpling.
He's now My Teddy Bear.
Maybe someday,
simply Teddy
or Ted
or he'll grow into a distinguished Theodore…
But whatever name that boy decides upon,
        there's a chef that brought him hence,
and loving hands
that primped
and tickled
and caressed
his little doughy cheeks.
And no matter what you'll come to call him,
        he'll always call me,
"Mom."

The Tale of Lora Lea

In the hollers of Appalachia,
whispers of neighbors still linger upon it—
    The Tale of Lora Lea.
Fingers of twilight tangle in a life of shadows,
where her pain was a dagger
    piercing souls beyond her own.
Her daughter's eyes forever seek an elusive,
fleeting, mother's love.
But in Lora Lea's gaze, a wild tempest brewed.
Those lifeless teal eyes, haunted,
    subdued dreams with what they'd seen.
Her auburn locks tressed a disheveled crown
and the laurels she wore over pain unseen
were the self-harm scars that swathed her arms.
Artistry and intelligence were dormant powers,
for shadows of trauma seized all promise long
ago.
She walked away from middle school halls,
forsaking her dreams from that day on.

The weight of her past was a burden too deep,
and it plagued her at night when she tossed in
her sheets.
In twilight hours,
with grapefruit and vodka,
she begged for escape,
from echoes and flashbacks
of the night she was raped.
But that daughter resulted,
and maintained tender heart,
just to see her mother's world crumbling apart.
Resentment brewed in Lora Lea's breast.
This child conceived in pain,
her resemblance an even crueler jest.
But love still lingered,
like fragile thread,
crocheted in words that would never be said.
Depression gripped her with its relentless hold.
Trauma whispered,
cruel and cold.
She etched bladed stripes upon her skin,
tattooing sorrow,
of stains seeping from within.
This daughter again, a nuisance in the night,
still seeking approval,
still craving light—
She will never be quite good enough.
The relentless ache to please
can never mend,

for it is nestled evermore
in the overhanging shadow of Lora Lea.
This bird has fallen from her nest.
          Her mother takes wing,
leaving her baby flightless on the ground.
But love still endures—despite her pain.
In the heart of a daughter,
love is profoundly engrained.
Yet there came a day when shadows won,
and Lora Lea's journey met with demise.
One fatal overdose,
          her weapon of choice,
                    ended her battle
through means swift and final.
Her act irrevocable,
wrenched apart those behind,
most especially the daughter
whose peace is long buried in the ashes.
In the nooks of that small country village,
neighbors' whispers still dwell…
Lora Lea's tale,
a bittersweet knell,
ever ringing on time,
almost as if summoned…
And in her daughter's heart,
she's living somewhere still,
a vision of Lora Lea that was never raped,
          a version that never walked away—
etched still with love, forever and a day.

Always

There's going to come a day when I have a
dollar to my name,
        and I've forgotten to pack my lunch,
when I called everyone and no one came,
        and I know you'll bring me brunch.
There will probably be another day when I wake
up with my hair a mess,
makeup still smudged from the late night before,
and I'm scrounging through laundry, last minute,
for a wrinkled dress.
You'll look me over and say, "You're beautiful.
Yes, I'm sure."
And another day, my car won't start.
I'll call you, and you'll lend your keys.
        Another, some jerk will break my heart.
You'll find him and douse him with hot grease.
And when there's broccoli stuck in my smile,
        or my shoelace is dragging the floor,
you won't wait and giggle a good long while.
You'll catch it before I'm out the door.
There will always be a day when I need you in
some way,
and every day that happens, I know you'll never
fail.
I just hope you realize that through each day,

my love's as strong as bitter black ale.
So, should there ever come a day you're too old
to change your sheets,
         you've forgotten my name or who I am,
when no one comes to your senior home's meet
'n greet…
I'll be the one checked in to hold your hand.

My Muse

In the void of blank pages, I sit dismayed,
My muse has fled; I need a better word than
dismayed.
With fingers poised and mind adrift,
I wrestle with words, but they're stiff as a thrift.

Anxiously checking *Submittable's* status, I pace.
I'm hoping for acceptance but fear disgrace.
Oh, the agony of this writer's plight,
lost in the darkness of non-creative night…

Should I adopt a pen name, I wonder?
Would it hide my shame or spark a thunder?
Perhaps "Quilliam Shakespeare" has a certain
ring,
or "J.D. Howdidthatsell" might have something
to bring.

Oh, to be like Rowling, scribbling success on
napkins…
But I struggle with plot holes and writing
mishaps happen.
E.L. James struck gold with fan-fiction smut,
yetI'm stuck in this rut, like some homeless mutt.

But amidst the chaos, there's a glimmer of hope.
It seems irony reigns in this writerly trope.
Though the struggle is real, success may yet shine
in the most unexpected ways; I will publish in time.

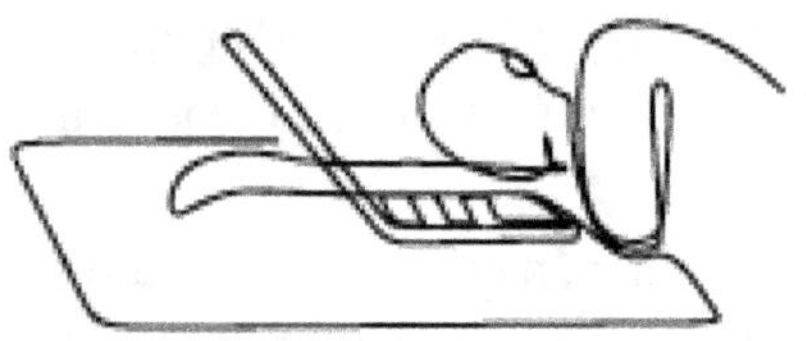

For Merri

In April's bloom, my daughter fair,
Merida graced the world with flair—
her locks like a raven feather's hue,
and eyes that twinkled merry and blue.
Shy she may be, in her tender years,
yet within her heart a melody appears.
Her voice, a sweet and gentle thing
like a bird in spring that takes to wing.
Three brothers strong, by her side they stand—
their bond unbreakable, hand in hand.
Together they roam, their hearts young and free,
in their world of wonder where dreams can be.
She leads their small pack as they dance and
sing
until the golden light of evening
reflects in Merida's eyes so bright.

I succumb to the joy of her exuberant light.
I love to cherish my daughter dear,
full of spirit, pure, and without fear.
For in Merida's embrace, I find
the beauty of innocence forever enshrined.

You Didn't Mean it

I passed a dead opossum on the road today.
      At least, it appeared to be…
I wanted to hope it was only playing.
Cars sped past, mindlessly zooming on their way
to work,
drivers in a hurry to update their *Excel* sheets
      and submit their inventory reports.
All this rush and anxiety—is this what we were
made for?
I passed the same spot on my way home from
work today.
I checked to see if that opossum was there.
My heart leapt at the empty space on the curb.
I drove on past, a small smile warming on my
face,

only to approach a sick plastering of blood and
organs a little way ahead.
      Her babies were there too.
Barely blinking in their mother's pouch—that's
all they were destined for.
Three babies and a mother died,
      all because some jerk was in a hurry
      on his way to a job he probably hates.
He will live the rest of his life never thinking of
this moment again.
Their poor little bodies, mangled and strewn
along the highway,
will eventually be nothing more than forgotten
stains
      washed away by a couple of good rains
and maybe even painted over when the city fixes
the road again.
The mother's heart within me broke.
I shuffled inside of my house, down, and hung
up my purse.
My partner gives me a hug, and asks, "Honey,
what's wrong?"
"Oh, nothing," I sigh.
      He knows better, but he doesn't pry.
He moves on and tells me about his day.
"I had a rough day too."
      "Oh?"
"Yeah, I hit an opossum on the way to work." I
froze.

"Poor little bugger. I tried to save her.
I got out of the car, but the traffic was insane.
I couldn't get to her before she got hit again."
I held him and rubbed his back.
"It's okay. You didn't mean it."
Thank God, it was an accident.
That's the nature of humanity—
to witness untold suffering to those around us
and tell ourselves and our loved ones that it's
okay, because
we didn't mean it.
But four more living beings would be here now
with a little care or mindfulness…
My partner will continue to speed.
I'm guilty of it too.
I guess sorry is as sorry does.

Bite Me

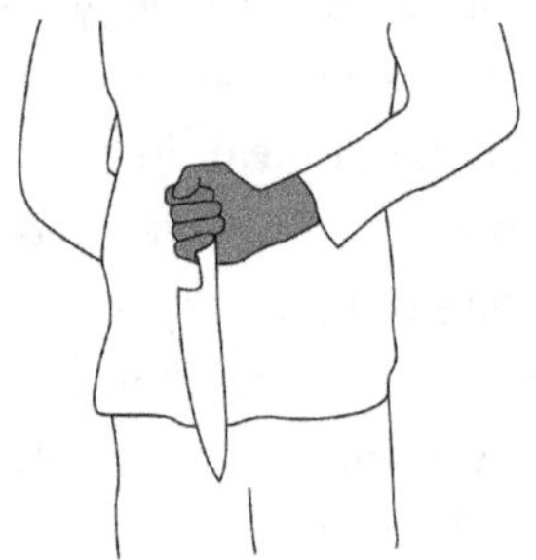

As long as I can remember, I have always loved animals,
from the cute cuddly kittens to the sleek, vicious scorpions.
I like them more than just about anyone.
I've always defended opossums, there's North America's only marsupial after all.
I think spiders are beautiful pets, whose molts are a form of art.
Pigs are not filthy eating machines; they're actually quite smart.
And so, seeing light in anyone and loving the unique nature of all species,
Naturally then, I assumed you were being maternal—
that your ever-hovering and guiding was a sign of care eternal.
When you bit me, I shook you off.

What are you doing? That hurts!
Then, you yelled at me when my blood spurt.
How dare I make this mess, even in my own
home—
  to do this in another's presence!
You told everyone I had no sense…
I even told you I was sorry,
as I looked down at the puncture wounds,
and I knew the relationship was ruined.
You slinked through the pool I left on the floor.
You wore my blood upon your skin like a fine
polish,
proud of the reputation you'd demolished.
Then, a piece of me I never knew existed, reared
its hurting head.
I called out the love I now knew was fake,
and then I called you, *my friend*, a snake.
I thought about it long and hard,
for snakes are cunning and they're beautiful,
  but isn't their primary goal survival?
I pity a creature that must kill to survive,
that lives with the memory of a heartbeat
stopping in its throat.
But I cannot pity a creature who does it to gloat.
As long as I can remember, I have always loved
animals,
  I was raised to love everyone.
I guess that's easier said than done.

Squirrel

In the tapestry of life there's a thread so rare—
a friend I've nicknamed Squirrel, who's always
been there.
Sable hair in a ponytail, eyes murky brown,
and under his frailty, a strength profound.

His olive skin tells tales of battles won,
yet his journey, we hope, is far from done.
Lanky frame and lacking grace,
but charming nonetheless. He holds a special
place.

Vigor's shadow wanes in a constant fight.
Still, he faces each day with all his might.
Sarcasm his armor, confrontation his song,
but beneath the bravado, his spirit is strong.

Outside all the lines, his mind is always in flight.
In the cosmos of thought, he seeks more insight.
String Theory's mysteries are a puzzle to solve.
In the night sky's whispers, he finds his resolve.

Comedy and metal are his heart's favorite beat.
In laughter and music, his joy is complete.
A lonely warrior in solitude's embrace,
but of friendship's warmth, he still craves grace.

He thinks too much; his mind a stormy sea
lost in introspection, longing to be free…
Yet in his depths lie wonders untold.
In his mental typhoon, unrivaled stories unfold.

Low self-esteem weighs heavy on his soul,
but in his presence, I feel whole.
For in Squirrel, I've found a friend so rare,
a bond unbreakable; love beyond compare.

From cradle to grave, our journey's intertwined.
Our laughter, our tears, our spirits aligned.
It's in Squirrel's presence, I find my home
in the roots of friendship, where we'll ever roam.

For Atréus

You grip my thumb like a life support,
as if I took it back, you might float away,
completely unaware that someday you'll want
to.
Every little robin must learn to fly.
My heart will sing for you, belting from the
mountaintops,
      but my arms will fall, dejected,
         empty without my baby bird.
There will come a day when I recline back on
my couch,
tirelessly quilting mismatched blankets
from clothes you've outgrown
and little baby towels I can't throw away.
There will come a day when I clean out your
room,

and I will gather your bath toys and say,
"This rubber ducky needs to stay."
I can't stop the day you'll leave.
I don't even want to, for *your* sake.
But I hope someday the little minutiae of you,
scattered about,
    will leave an impression—
      that a memory still jogs.
I'll find some sweater or a baby rattle,
I'll press it to my chest,
   and for a moment,
    it will be my life support.

My Stride

I've never smiled so big in all my life.
I graduated college;
I've had my romance;
I made beautiful children.
I punch the clock every day,
the model employee who always steps up when
needed.
I brush my hair and my teeth,
I soak in a bubble bath with my rubber duckies,
and I take a steaming hot shower after that.
My house is the cleanest it has ever been.
Color-coordinated and alphabetized,
every label faces forward and aligns
equidistantly.
I guess it seems I've hit my stride.
When I bumped into you today at the grocery
store,
and you asked me,
"Hey, how are you?"
I don't know what made me burst into tears.

Sure, I waited until I answered the socially acceptable,
"I'm doing great! You?"
But I scrambled for my car,
        and I sobbed an ugly, wallowing cry.
My kid's on the honor roll, my cats are fat and content.
Dinner's on the table, home-cooked and savory by my hand.
I'm paid up on my rent.
My car runs great, but I still have a spare.
The carpet is rough, but the floor beneath, sturdy.
I'm early in my thirties— they say this is my prime.
Isn't this my stride?
When I tucked my baby into sleep,
I turned out his light,
        and I rushed back to close my door.
I don't know what made me burst into tears.
Sure, I waited until he was snugly asleep,
but I scrambled through the medicine cabinet.
Allergies, eye drops, headache pills, and chews...
        but *none* of this would do.
Nothing here will take this pain.
Nothing here will end me for good.
Nothing here will clean up the mess of what could.

But, I've hit my stride.
I'm doing great! You?
I've never smiled so big in all my life.

Plunge

I didn't fall into these waters by accident.
I turned my back to the sea, I closed my eyes,
        and I plunged.
The water struck me like concrete,
smooth facade giving way to turbulent force,
forcing the air from my lungs.
With no skill to swim but a dreamy vision—
drifting away, serenely and trancelike,
reality's fury met me head-on.
A fierce God rebuked my recklessness,
 "How dare you?"
        He turned his face away.
The more I struggled against the massive waves,
        the more tired my arms became,

and the harder it was to meet each oncoming
crash.
I plowed into a colony of rocks and was struck
by another barrage from the tide.
       I wanted to move—really, I did!
           But I lost all control. I lost *me*.
Eventually exhausted by futile efforts against the
marine assault,
       I let myself succumb.
         It was only for a moment.
Before I knew it, the sky was black above me,
engulfed by a deep cavern of waves and debris.
My eyes filled up with stinging salt.
Some nearby bubbles teased hope, and I
swallowed them for air,
but it only hurt that much more to take the water
with it.
It had nothing else to do but fill my lungs.
I finally let go and tried to relax and float.
       My body flittered up just enough
that I saw a flickering flash of red—
            a floatation device—
              Salvation!
I found the urge to fight and struggled upward to
it,
greedily seizing the plastic with all I could
muster.
But then, I heard a scream.
I knew your voice, my love.

You'd jumped in to rescue me,
         though no stronger a swimmer than I.
So, I tossed the device to you.
"Take it!" I yelled, throwing it away with both
hands,
         watching your desperate eyes receive it.
I could tell you wanted to help.
         Truly, wholeheartedly, you did,
              but you *needed* to live.
We both knew this was my folly.
         Does it then stand that I deserve it?
Did I earn this pain I never could have imagined
for sheer ignorance?
I didn't fall into these waters by accident.
I turned my back to the sea, I closed my eyes,
         and I plunged.
When the tide dies down,
and my limbs and lungs finally cease their
struggle,
         will I find balm in Gilead?
Will I close my eyes forever,
or will I open them and fight with all my might?
Perhaps the lesson of leaping comes too late to
learn to swim.

Robotic Hearts

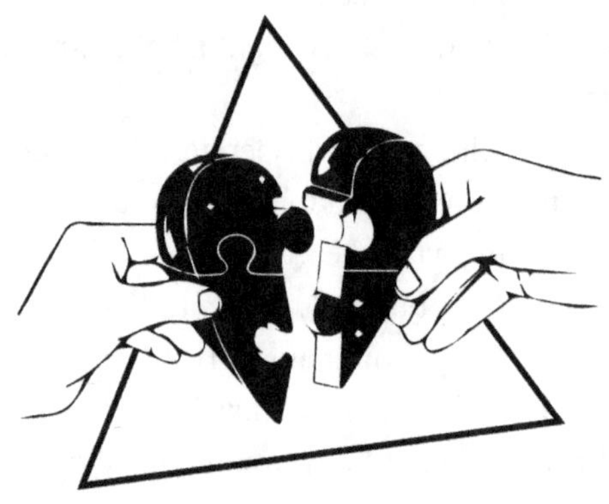

In circuits spun of flesh and bone,
robotic hearts in silence, drone.
With binary whispers, minds entwine,
all ones and zeros and thoughts confined.
Javascript tongues in human guise,
we speak our codes and print out demise.
But in this script, there's a line amiss,
a rhyme that fails—a gentle kiss.
"Does not compute," the line protests.
It's a glitch in the code, a misunderstood jest.
Through dry humor, we giggle and sigh.
With bytes of awkward gestures, we struggle to
comply.
Button mashing—our intimate dance—
this awkward step becomes romance.
Like coding errors, love's embrace,

our glitchy rhythm in time and space.
But in this world of wires and dreams
where humans hide in binary schemes,
we find these glitches, human art.
We find love beats our digital hearts.

Get to the Point

There's a phenomenon people refer to as
"talking in circles."
I speak in squares.
My words are rigid and concise.
They reach each point with purpose,
and find their way back to a common theme.
My words are not flowery prose and cursive
lines.
They aren't dually meant; their humor is dry.
  They mean exactly what they say.
My words and voice will never be used to
advertise,
like the monotonous but soothing tone of Ben
Stein.
They will seldom leave you laughing,
  and more often may leave you confused.
Their absolutes can be frustrating for you,
  as elusive nuance is to me.
But, my words have their place among the world
too.
The fluffiness of a lazy summer cloud
  or the plump pinkness of a baby's cheek
   is that much softer
because of the jagged, rigid fragments of the
world.

Pencils write better when they're sharpened.
Squared buildings are structured so to inspire
trust and power.
Bridges lead straight, swift, and safe.
I speak in squares.
I cannot fit my squared points into your round
plot.
Some people speak in heptagrams or triquetras,
excitement bursting and unfocused,
and they'll never fit into my square plot.
And that's okay too.

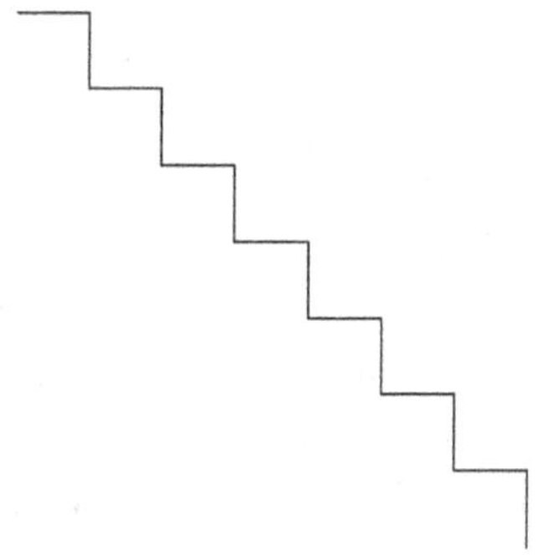

Tales of the Night

In the quiet of night, a *Pooh Bear* nightlight
aglow,
four beloved little hearts in dreaming, doze.
Through the stillness, my gray eyes hold their
tears.
Now that my loves sleep, despair draws near.

Three jobs I toil, under the weight of strife.
A single mother, I carve life from the knife.
In the kitchen's welcome, my sanctuary I find
cooking love into each dinner if just to unwind.

In words, my solace whispers sweet release
writing these books where I find fleeting peace.
Yet the shadows linger, haunting my mind,
with echoes of a past I struggle to leave behind.

Edgar Allan Poe's tales, a darkened mirror,
reflect the very depths of my own interior.
And Stephen King, with horrors writ untold,
a mirror to the terrors my own soul holds.

Depression's grip, a relentless tide,
and scars of trauma, where demons hide.
The future, a distant dim-lit shore,

seems to promise little but sorrow evermore.

Yet, within this darkness, a flicker burns bright;
The love for my children, a guiding light.
With each day's struggle, I press on anew
for their sake, for love, for dreams yet to
pursue…

So, though the road ahead may seem unkind,
in the love of my children, hope I still find.
Through love, support, writing, and tales of the
night,
I navigate darkness, chasing glimpses of light.

The Standard 2.5

Having a child is always such a blessing.
Congratulations! When are you due?
Oh, I am so happy for you!
Having your second child is even better.
How wonderful, So-and-So will finally be a
brother!
Do you think you'll want anymore?
But there's a shift in having your third child.
You know what causes that, right?
Are you going to get fixed after this one?
They say "get fixed" as if I'm a dog needing
spay.
The *average* American household estimates an
average number of 2.5 children per household.
We all know only *average* is acceptable.

Three children is that uncomfortable point when
you've passed the bar,
but some people are still willing to accept the
average rounded up.
There's another territory though, when a mother
has her fourth child, or beyond.
It happens when we file ourselves into an
elevator, trying not to occupy its entire space.
I hold my babies close to me,
and I squeeze their tiny shoulders when some
annoyed stranger whispers,
  "And I bet they're all on Welfare too."
    Another stranger snickers back.
Another shakes his head and says, "Stay off her,
man."
Now, that's just too many. I could never do that.
My tiny miracles look up at me, blue eyes
confused,
  wondering which of them are mistakes.
Which of them is the straw that breaks the
camel's back?
Is it my oldest, conceived through donation and
so genetically different,
when I was diagnosed infertile
after seven years of trying?
Perhaps my second-oldest, whom was a last
chance fertility treatment effort
when I cried over negative tests for two years
  trying to give my oldest a brother?

Or what about my daughter, the only girl,
          sticking out like a sore thumb
                    against the pack of all my boys?
Or is it my youngest baby boy,
          the one who broke the societal norm,
and could not be justified by rounding the
average up?
Each one of them so precious and so loved,
how could I *ever* allow them to believe they're a
mistake?
          How can you?
Having a child should always be a blessing.
          Congratulations! When are you due?
                    Oh, I am so happy for you!
Nothing more.
Nothing less.

Chrysalis

When I was just an egg posted on a leaf,
I rolled around and found my mother gone.
> I rolled,
>> and I rolled,
>>> and one day,

I hatched.
It was scary starting over.
The life of a caterpillar is harsh.
> All it would take is one cold, bitter day
or some larger creature to mark me his prey…
I should have noticed you from a mile away.
You picked me up and placed me in your palm.
> It was warm.
Your heart beat against my brown fuzz.
> I curled into you, safe at last.
And out of nowhere, you flicked me away.
> "Gross!" You shouted,
>> as my squishy form hit the tree.
It was such a shock, I wasn't sure I was still me.
Oh, how I missed the warmth of your hand,
every bit as much as I missed my mother too.
> I was abandoned once more.
I puffed out my spines and dared anyone to
approach me ever again.

It isn't that I wasn't lonely, but it just wasn't my
time.
My time was to hide; My time was to heal.
I curled up in camouflage, spun myself a thread,
          and I attached it to a twig.
It was there I waited,
          contemplated,
                    and pupated…
                              until I turned to mush.
It was here, in my most vulnerable state,
the place where everything that symbolized me
degraded,
          that something woke inside my soul.
The time was tedious, but I felt an evolution in
me.
An energy was rumbling, and I felt a new thing
stretch forth.
Out of the chrysalis, I see my first wing,
a stunning, intricate pattern—*all mine*—and
fluttering.
Fast and flittering, I can hardly contain my
excitement,
          for if just in this moment,
                    I am beautiful.
It's one of those lessons that cannot be simply
told.
My value was not determined when my mother
left me

anymore than it was when you cradled me and
flicked me away.
My value came from surviving the elements and
all who hurt me,
        to spring forth a winged goddess
                that you will *never* touch again,
and you can only *hope* to view.